AI Real Estate Financing & Loan Strategies

How to Use AI to Find the Best Mortgage, DSCR, and Funding Options

By Joe Correa

Published by Live Stronger Faster

This book is for educational and informational purposes only. The author and publisher are not engaged in rendering legal, financial, or other professional advice. Readers should consult a qualified professional before making any financial decisions.

First Edition

Table of Contents

Introduction 5

Chapter 1: The New Era of AI Loan Comparison and Financing Intelligence 11

Chapter 2: DSCR, Non-QM, and AI-Driven Qualification Strategy 20

Chapter 3: HELOC Strategy, Capital Recycling, and AI-Driven Leverage Optimization 30

Chapter 4: Prequalification Intelligence and AI-Powered Approval Strategy 39

Chapter 5: Borrower Optimization and AI-Driven Financial Positioning 49

Chapter 6: AI Timing Strategy, Rate Cycles, and Market-Driven Financing Decisions 60

Chapter 7: AI Portfolio-Level Financing Systems and Scalable Capital Architecture 70

Chapter 8: AI Financing Ecosystem Design and the Future of Autonomous Real Estate Capital 80

Chapter 9: AI Portfolio Management, Automation Systems, and Scalable Real Estate Operations 91

Chapter 10: The Fully Autonomous AI Real Estate Empire – Building a Self-Running Wealth System............................101

Final Comments.. 111

Introduction

The evolution of real estate investing does not stop at finding deals, analyzing properties, or even optimizing rental income. The real leverage point—the stage where most investors either accelerate into scale or get stuck—is financing. Capital determines speed. Capital determines flexibility. And ultimately, capital determines how many opportunities you can actually act on instead of just analyzing. Book 8 marks a critical transition in this entire AI Real Estate Investing Series, because it moves beyond deal discovery and property performance into the engine that powers everything behind the scenes: funding, structuring, and strategically leveraging money. Artificial intelligence is now transforming this space in ways that were previously only available to institutional investors, private equity firms, and highly connected real estate operators. Today, even individual investors can use AI to compare loan products, structure deals, and optimize borrowing decisions with a level of clarity and speed that was simply not possible before.

At its core, AI Real Estate Financing is about decision intelligence. In traditional investing, financing decisions were often reactive. Investors would speak to a lender, receive limited options, and choose based on incomplete information or time pressure. Many deals were lost not because they were bad deals, but because funding took too long, terms were misunderstood, or the investor simply did not know better alternatives existed. Now, with AI systems, financing becomes proactive, strategic, and data-driven. Instead of asking "Can I get approved?", the modern investor begins asking "What is the optimal way to structure this deal for maximum cash flow, lowest risk, and fastest scaling potential?" AI helps bridge this gap by evaluating multiple loan scenarios simultaneously, identifying hidden advantages in different lending programs, and aligning financing strategies with long-term portfolio goals.

One of the most powerful transformations in this space is the rise of AI-assisted loan comparison. Investors are no longer limited to one or two lender conversations. With AI tools, it is now possible to simulate multiple financing structures side by side. Conventional loans, DSCR loans, Non-QM products, HELOC strategies, private lending, and hybrid funding approaches can all be evaluated in seconds. This allows investors to understand not just the interest rate, but the full financial impact of each option, including cash flow, equity position, amortization effects, refinance potential, and long-term wealth implications. Instead of guessing, investors can now model outcomes before ever submitting an application. This dramatically reduces risk and increases confidence when making high-stakes decisions. Another major shift comes from the use of AI in DSCR and income-based financing strategies. Debt Service Coverage Ratio loans, which are especially popular among rental investors, rely heavily on property income rather than personal income. AI tools can now estimate rental income, analyze market comparables, and predict DSCR ratios with increasing accuracy. This means investors can pre-evaluate whether a property will qualify before even making an offer. It eliminates wasted time and allows for faster, more strategic acquisitions. In addition, AI can optimize DSCR structures by suggesting down payment adjustments, interest rate scenarios, and rental pricing strategies that improve qualification odds while still maintaining profitability.

Non-QM lending, which includes bank statement loans, asset-based loans, and other alternative documentation programs, is another area where AI is becoming extremely valuable. These loan types are often misunderstood or underutilized because they are complex and vary widely between lenders. AI simplifies this complexity by mapping borrower profiles against lender guidelines, identifying the most suitable programs, and highlighting qualification pathways that might not be obvious through traditional channels. For self-employed investors, business owners, and high-net-worth individuals, this creates massive opportunity because income documentation is no longer a barrier—it becomes a variable that can be strategically positioned. Perhaps one of the most impactful applications of AI in financing is HELOC strategy optimization. Home Equity Lines of Credit have become one of the most powerful tools for real estate investors because they allow capital recycling. However, most investors underutilize them or misunderstand how to integrate them into larger investment strategies. AI can now evaluate equity positions, compare HELOC terms across multiple lenders, and recommend draw strategies based on investment timelines. For example, AI can help determine whether it is more effective to use a HELOC for down payments on multiple properties, to renovate existing assets, or to act as a liquidity buffer for opportunistic acquisitions. This transforms HELOCs from simple credit lines into dynamic investment engines.

Prequalification automation is another key advancement reshaping the financing process. Traditionally, prequalification required manual document submission, back-and-forth communication, and waiting periods that slowed down deal execution. AI now streamlines this process by analyzing borrower profiles, income structures, credit profiles, and asset positions to predict approval likelihood before formal submission. This allows investors to focus only on viable deals and avoid wasting time on financing paths that are unlikely to succeed. It also enables faster decision-making in competitive markets where speed is often the difference between securing a property or losing it to another buyer. Borrower optimization is an emerging concept that is fundamentally changing how investors present themselves to lenders. Instead of passively submitting financial documents, investors can now use AI to strategically optimize their financial presentation. This does not mean altering or misrepresenting information, but rather understanding how different lenders evaluate risk and structuring applications in the most favorable way possible. AI can identify which income sources carry more weight, how debt-to-income ratios are interpreted differently across lenders, and how asset reserves impact approval strength. This level of insight used to be reserved for experienced mortgage professionals and underwriters. Now it is becoming accessible to any investor willing to leverage technology.

As we move deeper into this new era, financing is no longer a separate step in the investment process. It becomes fully integrated with acquisition strategy, property analysis, and portfolio planning. The investor is no longer just a buyer of real estate. They become a capital strategist, using AI as a tool to constantly evaluate leverage opportunities and optimize returns across multiple properties. Every deal becomes part of a larger system rather than an isolated transaction. Financing decisions begin to compound just like investment returns, creating exponential advantages over time.

This book will explore not only the tools and systems behind AI-driven financing, but also the mindset shift required to use them effectively. Because the true power of AI in real estate financing is not just automation—it is intelligence amplification. It allows investors to think bigger, act faster, and structure deals in ways that were previously too complex or time-consuming to execute. The result is a more efficient, more scalable, and more resilient investment portfolio.

Throughout the chapters ahead, we will break down how AI compares loan products, how DSCR and Non-QM strategies can be optimized, how HELOCs can be transformed into investment capital engines, and how prequalification systems can dramatically increase deal velocity. You will also learn how to align financing decisions with long-term wealth-building strategies, ensuring that every loan, every structure, and every funding decision contributes to your broader financial goals rather than limiting them.

By the end of this book, financing will no longer feel like a constraint or a bottleneck. Instead, it will become one of your greatest strategic advantages. You will understand how to use AI not just to get approved, but to get optimized. Not just to fund deals, but to structure them intelligently. And not just to borrow money, but to build a scalable system of capital that fuels continuous real estate growth.

Chapter 1

The New Era of AI Loan Comparison and Financing Intelligence

Financing has always been the hidden engine behind real estate investing, but for most investors it has also been the most limiting factor. Deals are often found too late, capital is structured too slowly, or lending options are misunderstood until the opportunity has already passed. In traditional real estate investing, financing was treated as a separate step—something that happens after the deal is found. However, in the modern AI-driven environment, financing is no longer a separate step. It is integrated directly into the decision-making process from the very beginning. This shift fundamentally changes how investors evaluate opportunities, because the question is no longer simply whether a property is a good deal, but whether it can be optimally financed in a way that maximizes returns and minimizes long-term risk.

Artificial intelligence introduces a level of clarity into loan comparison that previously required years of experience or access to multiple lenders and brokers. Instead of relying on a single loan officer's perspective, investors can now simulate multiple financing scenarios instantly. Conventional mortgages, DSCR loans, Non-QM programs, asset-based lending, HELOC structures, and hybrid financing strategies can all be evaluated side by side. This is not just about comparing interest rates. It is about understanding the full financial architecture of a deal—cash flow impact, amortization schedules, equity positioning, refinancing potential, and long-term scalability.

One of the most powerful applications of AI in financing is its ability to interpret borrower profiles in real time. By analyzing income structure, credit profile, debt obligations, and asset reserves, AI systems can predict which loan programs are most likely to approve a borrower before a formal application is submitted. This removes uncertainty and significantly reduces wasted time. Instead of applying blindly to multiple lenders, investors can strategically target only those financing options that align with their profile and investment goals. This shift alone dramatically increases efficiency in deal execution.

Another critical advantage of AI loan comparison is its ability to model outcomes beyond the surface-level terms of a loan. Most investors traditionally focus on interest rate, down payment, and monthly payment. However, AI systems go deeper by evaluating how each loan structure impacts long-term wealth accumulation. For example, a slightly higher interest rate might actually result in better cash flow if it allows for a lower down payment or improved leverage.

Similarly, a loan with higher upfront costs might create greater long-term equity acceleration if paired with the right property strategy. AI brings these hidden relationships to the surface, allowing investors to make decisions based on total financial impact rather than isolated variables.

DSCR loans represent one of the most important financing tools in this new ecosystem. These loans evaluate properties based on their income-generating ability rather than the borrower's personal income. AI enhances DSCR analysis by accurately estimating rental income using market data, comparable properties, seasonal trends, and occupancy assumptions. Instead of relying on rough estimates or conservative lender assumptions, investors can now pre-calculate DSCR ratios with far greater precision. This allows them to adjust offers, rental strategies, or down payments before committing to a purchase. The result is a significantly higher approval rate and fewer surprises during underwriting.

Non-QM lending adds another layer of opportunity, especially for self-employed borrowers and investors with non-traditional income structures. These loans include bank statement programs, asset-based lending, and flexible documentation options. The complexity of Non-QM products often makes them difficult to navigate, but AI simplifies the process by matching borrower profiles with lender guidelines across multiple institutions. This creates a map of eligibility that highlights not only whether a borrower qualifies, but also which lender offers the most favorable structure for their specific financial situation. This level of optimization was previously only available to high-end mortgage professionals with deep industry knowledge.

HELOC strategies are also being transformed through AI-powered optimization. A Home Equity Line of Credit is no longer just a simple borrowing tool—it becomes a dynamic capital allocation system. AI evaluates existing equity positions, interest rates, draw schedules, and investment timelines to recommend how and when to use available credit. For example, an investor may be advised to use a HELOC for down payments on multiple properties while simultaneously maintaining liquidity for renovations or market opportunities. AI can also simulate repayment strategies, helping investors understand how different usage patterns affect long-term equity growth and risk exposure.

Prequalification automation is another major breakthrough in financing efficiency. Traditionally, prequalification required manual document submission and back-and-forth communication with lenders. Now, AI systems can analyze financial data instantly and generate prequalification insights in seconds. This allows investors to quickly determine whether a deal is financeable before spending time on underwriting processes. It also allows for faster decision-making in competitive markets where speed is critical. Investors who use AI-driven prequalification gain a significant advantage because they can move decisively while others are still waiting for lender feedback.

Borrower optimization represents one of the most strategic applications of AI in this entire ecosystem. Rather than passively submitting financial documents, investors can actively structure their financial profile in a way that aligns with lender expectations. AI can identify which income streams are most favorable, how debt ratios are interpreted across different institutions, and how asset reserves influence approval strength. This does not involve manipulation, but rather strategic presentation of financial information within legal and ethical guidelines. The result is stronger approvals, better terms, and more predictable lending outcomes.

As AI continues to evolve, financing is becoming less of a barrier and more of a strategic advantage. Investors are no longer constrained by limited lender relationships or incomplete information. Instead, they operate within a system where multiple financing pathways can be evaluated instantly, optimized continuously, and aligned directly with investment goals. This creates a new class of investor—one who thinks in systems rather than transactions, and who uses capital not just to buy properties, but to accelerate portfolio growth intelligently.

The future of real estate financing is not about finding money. It is about designing capital structures that adapt to opportunity. AI makes this possible by turning fragmented financial decisions into a unified system of intelligence. In this system, every loan is not just a funding mechanism, but a strategic component of a larger wealth-building engine.

"The Deal That Changed Everything"

Marcus had been investing in real estate for five years, but it always felt like he was running uphill. He could find deals. He could analyze them. He could even negotiate well. But when it came to financing, everything slowed down. Banks gave him inconsistent answers, lenders took too long to respond, and by the time he understood his options, the best deals were already gone.

One afternoon, while scrolling through investment forums, he kept seeing one phrase repeated over and over: AI loan comparison. At first, he dismissed it as another tech buzzword. But the more he read, the more he realized something important was changing in the industry. Investors were no longer relying on a single lender's opinion. They were using AI systems to evaluate multiple financing structures instantly.

Curious, Marcus decided to try it. He entered his financial profile into an AI platform powered by ChatGPT and a mortgage calculation engine similar to a modern Mortgage Calculator. Within seconds, the system analyzed his income, credit, assets, and debt structure. Then it presented him with something he had never seen before: five different financing strategies for the same property he was considering.

One option was a conventional loan with a low rate but high down payment. Another was a DSCR loan that qualified based on rental income. A third was a Non-QM bank statement loan tailored to his self-employed income. The fourth was a HELOC-based strategy that allowed him to leverage existing equity. And the fifth was a hybrid structure combining short-term financing with a refinance plan six months later.

Marcus sat back in disbelief. For the first time, financing wasn't confusing. It was visual. It was structured. It was clear.

He focused on a duplex in a growing neighborhood. Traditionally, he would have gone straight to a bank and hoped for approval. Instead, the AI showed him something unexpected. The DSCR loan option actually produced better monthly cash flow than the conventional loan, even though the interest rate was slightly higher. The reason was simple: lower down payment meant more capital preserved for future deals.

Even more surprising was the HELOC strategy. The AI showed him that by tapping into his home equity, he could purchase two properties instead of one, while still maintaining a safe reserve buffer. It even projected his portfolio growth over three years based on different financing combinations.

For the first time in his investing career, Marcus didn't feel limited by money. He felt guided by strategy.

He chose the DSCR structure for the duplex but combined it with a HELOC strategy for his next acquisition. The loan process was faster than anything he had experienced before. Because he already understood the financing path, there were no surprises, no delays, and no confusion.

Six months later, he stood in front of two cash-flowing properties instead of one. The difference wasn't luck. It wasn't timing. It wasn't even the deal itself.

It was financing intelligence.

Marcus realized something powerful that day. The investors who win in the next era of real estate won't just be the ones who find the best deals. They will be the ones who understand how to structure capital faster, smarter, and more strategically than everyone else.

And for Marcus, that shift began the moment he stopped thinking about loans as obstacles—and started using AI to turn them into opportunities.

Chapter 2

DSCR, Non-QM, and AI-Driven Qualification Strategy

Once investors begin to understand AI-powered loan comparison, the next evolution is learning how financing actually *qualifies* in today's lending environment. Chapter 1 focused on choosing between loan options. Chapter 2 goes deeper into something more powerful: how AI reshapes the way borrowers qualify for DSCR, Non-QM, and alternative financing structures that are rapidly becoming the backbone of modern real estate investing. This shift is important because qualification is no longer just a fixed set of rules. It is now a dynamic system influenced by property income, borrower structure, documentation strategy, and lender-specific guidelines that vary widely across the industry.

Traditionally, mortgage qualification was centered around personal income. W-2s, tax returns, and debt-to-income ratios determined access to financing. For many investors, especially self-employed individuals, this created friction and limitations that slowed portfolio growth. DSCR loans fundamentally changed this model by shifting the focus from borrower income to property income. Instead of asking "How much do you earn?", lenders began asking "Does the property generate enough income to cover its debt obligations?" This single shift opened the door to a much broader group of investors who were previously constrained by traditional underwriting models.

Artificial intelligence enhances DSCR lending by making income projection far more accurate and adaptive. Instead of relying on static rental assumptions, AI systems analyze market-level data, comparable rentals, occupancy trends, seasonal demand patterns, and historical pricing behavior. This allows investors to estimate DSCR ratios before ever submitting a loan application. In practice, this means investors can evaluate whether a property will qualify *before they even make an offer*, which dramatically reduces wasted time and failed underwriting attempts.

AI also helps optimize DSCR outcomes by adjusting variables in real time. For example, a slight change in down payment can significantly improve a DSCR ratio. Similarly, adjusting rental pricing strategy or selecting a different loan term can shift a property from "barely qualifying" to "strong approval category." Instead of guessing these outcomes, investors can simulate them instantly. This transforms DSCR lending from a reactive process into a proactive strategy where qualification is engineered rather than discovered. Beyond DSCR loans, Non-QM financing introduces an even more flexible set of options for investors who do not fit traditional lending molds. Non-QM (Non-Qualified Mortgage) products include bank statement loans, asset-based loans, interest-only programs, and other alternative documentation structures. These loans are designed for borrowers who may have strong financial capacity but non-traditional income documentation. Business owners, entrepreneurs, real estate investors, and high-net-worth individuals often fall into this category.

The complexity of Non-QM lending lies in its variability. Each lender has its own interpretation of risk, documentation requirements, and qualification thresholds. This is where AI becomes extremely powerful. By analyzing borrower profiles and comparing them against multiple lender guidelines, AI can identify the most suitable financing pathways in seconds. Instead of manually contacting multiple lenders, investors receive a ranked list of optimal lending options based on their specific financial situation.

For example, one lender may heavily favor bank statement deposits while another prioritizes asset reserves. Another may allow higher debt ratios if compensating factors are strong. AI systems detect these subtle differences and match them to borrower profiles. This creates a level of precision that was previously only available to highly experienced mortgage brokers or underwriters who understood lender behavior at a deep level. One of the most overlooked advantages of AI in Non-QM lending is borrower optimization. Borrower optimization is the process of structuring financial documentation in a way that aligns with lender interpretation models. This does not involve altering financial truth, but rather presenting information strategically within acceptable guidelines. AI can identify which income streams carry the most weight, how deposits should be categorized, and how asset reserves impact approval strength across different lenders.

This becomes especially powerful for self-employed borrowers who often have fluctuating income patterns. AI can analyze business cash flow trends, identify consistent income patterns that lenders are likely to accept, and recommend the best documentation strategy. In some cases, it may suggest using bank statements instead of tax returns, or combining asset reserves with income verification to strengthen the application. This level of insight dramatically improves approval odds and reduces uncertainty in the lending process.

Another major transformation is happening in the way AI handles prequalification. Instead of waiting days or weeks for lender feedback, investors can now receive instant prequalification assessments based on simulated underwriting models. AI evaluates income, credit, assets, and property data simultaneously, then predicts approval probability with a high degree of accuracy. This allows investors to eliminate weak deals early and focus only on transactions that are financeable.

Prequalification intelligence also enhances speed in competitive markets. Real estate is often a race against time, and financing delays can result in lost opportunities. With AI-driven prequalification, investors can confidently make offers knowing that financing has already been stress-tested against multiple lending scenarios. This reduces friction in negotiations and increases the likelihood of successful deal execution.

HELOC integration plays a significant role in both DSCR and Non-QM strategies. Home Equity Lines of Credit are often used as flexible capital sources for down payments, renovations, or bridge financing. AI helps investors determine the most effective way to deploy HELOC capital based on timing, interest rates, and investment return projections. In some cases, it may be more efficient to use HELOC funds for multiple smaller acquisitions rather than a single large investment. In other cases, it may be strategically better to reserve HELOC capacity for renovation cycles or market downturn opportunities.

What makes AI particularly powerful in HELOC strategy is its ability to simulate long-term capital recycling. Investors can see how using equity today impacts future borrowing capacity, portfolio expansion speed, and overall risk exposure. This creates a feedback loop where capital decisions are no longer isolated events but part of an ongoing financial system.

As DSCR, Non-QM, and HELOC strategies converge, investors begin to operate within a unified financing ecosystem. Instead of thinking in terms of individual loans, they begin thinking in terms of capital cycles. Each property becomes part of a larger financial structure where equity is continuously recycled, debt is strategically managed, and cash flow is optimized across multiple assets.

AI is what makes this level of coordination possible. Without it, investors would need to manually track multiple lenders, constantly recalculate ratios, and manage complex documentation processes. With it, financing becomes centralized, intelligent, and adaptive. It evolves as the investor's portfolio evolves.

Ultimately, the purpose of this chapter is to shift the investor's mindset. Financing is not a hurdle to overcome—it is a system to be optimized. DSCR loans remove income barriers, Non-QM loans remove documentation limitations, and AI removes guesswork. Together, they create a financing environment where decisions are no longer reactive but strategically engineered for scale.

The investors who understand this shift are not just buying properties. They are building financial systems that compound over time, where every loan strengthens the next opportunity, and every financing decision becomes part of a larger wealth-building structure.

"The Borrower Who Stopped Guessing"

Daniel had always believed he was a strong investor. He knew how to find properties, run basic numbers, and negotiate deals. But every time he reached the financing stage, everything slowed down. He would submit applications, wait for responses, send documents back and forth, and still feel uncertain about whether he was getting the best structure. Deals slipped through his fingers not because of lack of opportunity, but because of delays in financing clarity.

One evening, frustrated after losing a duplex deal he had worked on for weeks, Daniel decided to try something different. He had heard other investors mention AI-based financing tools that could analyze DSCR and Non-QM loan options. Skeptical but curious, he entered his financial profile, property details, and investment goals into an AI system powered by advanced lending models similar to ChatGPT and mortgage analysis engines.

Within moments, the system generated something he had never experienced before: a complete financing map. It showed him a DSCR loan option that qualified based entirely on projected rental income. It showed a bank statement loan that used his business deposits instead of tax returns. It showed a HELOC-based strategy using equity from his primary residence. And it even showed a hybrid approach that combined short-term financing with a refinance strategy after stabilization.

Daniel was stunned. For the first time, financing wasn't a mystery—it was a system.

He focused again on the duplex he had lost. The AI showed him something critical. The reason he lost the deal wasn't price. It was timing. The lender he originally approached took too long to evaluate his income documentation. But under a DSCR structure, the property would have qualified instantly based on projected rental income.

Even more surprising, the AI showed him that if he had used a HELOC for the down payment instead of liquidating savings, he could have moved faster and still maintained liquidity for future deals. The difference was not just approval—it was strategy.

Daniel realized he had been thinking about financing incorrectly his entire investing career. He thought of it as something you "apply for." The AI showed him it was something you "design." Over the next few weeks, Daniel began restructuring his entire approach. Before analyzing deals, he would run financing simulations first. He learned how DSCR ratios shifted with small changes in rent assumptions. He learned how Non-QM lenders interpreted bank deposits differently. He learned how HELOC timing affected portfolio expansion speed.

Then came the turning point.

A new property hit the market—a small fourplex in an area he knew well. In the past, he would have rushed to apply for financing and hoped for approval. This time, he paused. He ran it through the AI system first.

Within seconds, he saw the optimal structure. A DSCR loan with a slightly higher interest rate but significantly lower down payment, allowing him to preserve capital. The system also showed him that pairing it with a HELOC draw would allow him to prepare for a second acquisition within 60 days.

For the first time, Daniel wasn't guessing.

He made the offer. It was accepted.

This time, financing didn't slow him down. It accelerated him.

Thirty days later, he closed the deal. No delays. No confusion. No surprises. As he stood inside one of the units, he realized something simple but powerful: the difference between his past failures and his current success wasn't effort. It was intelligence.

Not just his own intelligence—but the intelligence of the system he was now using.

Daniel was no longer chasing approvals.

He was designing them.

Chapter 3

HELOC Strategy, Capital Recycling, and AI-Driven Leverage Optimization

Once an investor understands DSCR and Non-QM lending, the next evolution in AI-powered real estate financing is learning how to actively control and recycle capital. This is where HELOC strategies become one of the most powerful tools in an investor's entire financial toolkit. A Home Equity Line of Credit is often misunderstood as a simple backup funding source or emergency reserve. In reality, when combined with AI-driven analysis, it becomes a dynamic capital engine that can accelerate portfolio growth, increase liquidity, and reduce dependency on traditional lending cycles. The key shift is understanding that HELOCs are not static debt instruments—they are flexible, reusable capital systems.

Traditionally, investors used HELOCs reactively. They would pull equity when cash was needed, often without a structured repayment or reinvestment strategy. This reactive behavior limited the true potential of leverage. AI changes this entirely by transforming HELOC usage into a predictive and strategic process. Instead of asking "Can I borrow against my home?", the investor now asks "How can I optimize my equity position across multiple investments over time?" AI evaluates current property equity, interest rates, draw schedules, and projected investment returns to recommend the most efficient use of available capital.

One of the most important advancements in AI-driven HELOC strategy is capital allocation modeling. AI systems can simulate multiple scenarios where HELOC funds are deployed across different investment opportunities. For example, one scenario might allocate equity toward a single high-cash-flow property. Another might distribute capital across multiple smaller acquisitions. A third might reserve funds for renovation cycles or opportunistic market entry. By comparing these scenarios, investors gain clarity on not only what they *can* do, but what they *should* do based on long-term portfolio performance.

This is where the concept of capital recycling becomes essential. Capital recycling is the process of using borrowed funds to acquire assets, generating income or equity growth from those assets, and then reusing that capital again for additional investments. In traditional investing, this process was slow and manual. Investors would often wait years before refinancing or accessing equity again. With AI, this cycle becomes continuous and optimized. The system can project when equity will be available, how refinancing will impact cash flow, and when the next investment opportunity should be triggered. Another critical function of AI in HELOC strategy is timing optimization. Timing is one of the most overlooked aspects of leverage. Drawing equity too early can increase risk exposure, while waiting too long can result in missed opportunities. AI helps solve this by analyzing market conditions, interest rate environments, rental demand cycles, and property appreciation trends. Based on this data, it can recommend optimal draw timing and repayment strategies that align with both market conditions and investor goals.

AI also enhances HELOC risk management in ways that were previously unavailable to individual investors. Leverage inherently carries risk, especially when multiple properties are financed simultaneously. AI systems can model worst-case scenarios, including interest rate increases, rental market declines, or unexpected vacancy periods. By simulating these conditions, investors can understand how much leverage is safe to deploy at any given time. This transforms HELOC usage from speculative borrowing into calculated financial engineering.

One of the most powerful applications of HELOC optimization is down payment stacking. Instead of relying on savings or liquidating assets, investors can strategically use equity from existing properties to fund new acquisitions. AI can calculate how much equity can be safely extracted without jeopardizing portfolio stability. It can also determine whether it is more efficient to use HELOC funds for down payments, renovations, or acquisition costs. This level of precision allows investors to scale faster without overextending financially.

Another major advantage of AI-driven HELOC strategy is cross-property leverage balancing. Many investors unknowingly create uneven exposure across their portfolios by concentrating debt in certain areas or properties. AI identifies these imbalances and recommends adjustments to maintain healthy leverage ratios. This might include refinancing certain properties, reallocating equity, or adjusting repayment schedules. The goal is not just growth, but sustainable growth that minimizes systemic risk.

When combined with DSCR and Non-QM financing strategies, HELOC optimization becomes even more powerful. For example, an investor might use a HELOC to fund a down payment on a DSCR property, which then generates rental income that improves their overall portfolio cash flow. That cash flow can then be used to qualify for additional Non-QM loans, which expand purchasing power further. AI connects these strategies into a unified system, allowing each financing decision to support the next.

This interconnected structure is what separates traditional

investors from AI-powered investors. In traditional models, each loan is treated as an isolated event. In AI-driven models, every loan is part of a larger capital ecosystem. HELOCs, DSCR loans, Non-QM financing, and cash flow reinvestment all become interconnected components of a continuous growth cycle. The investor is no longer managing individual transactions—they are managing a financial system.

AI also plays a critical role in repayment strategy optimization. Many investors make the mistake of treating HELOCs as long-term debt without a clear repayment plan. AI can design repayment structures based on cash flow projections, rental income cycles, and refinancing opportunities. In some cases, it may recommend aggressive repayment to restore borrowing capacity quickly. In other cases, it may suggest maintaining minimal payments to preserve liquidity for additional investments. The strategy is always dynamic and tailored to portfolio behavior.

As investors scale, HELOC strategy becomes less about individual loans and more about liquidity architecture. Liquidity architecture refers to the way capital flows through an investment portfolio over time. AI helps design this architecture by mapping how funds move between properties, loans, and reinvestment cycles. This creates a financial ecosystem where capital is constantly circulating rather than sitting idle. Ultimately, HELOC optimization is about control. It gives investors the ability to decide when, how, and where capital is deployed. Combined with AI, this control becomes precise, adaptive, and scalable. Instead of reacting to opportunities with limited resources, investors proactively create opportunities by strategically positioning capital in advance.

The result is a shift in mindset. Borrowing is no longer seen as debt accumulation. It becomes a tool for acceleration. Equity is no longer static wealth. It becomes active fuel for expansion. And financing is no longer a constraint. It becomes a system of controlled leverage that compounds over time.

This chapter represents a turning point in the investor journey. Once HELOC strategy is understood at this level, real estate investing stops being about individual property decisions and becomes about designing a self-sustaining financial engine.

"The Equity That Built an Empire"

Lena had always been careful with money. She worked hard, saved consistently, and eventually paid down significant equity in her primary home and two rental properties. On paper, she was doing everything right. But despite her financial stability, her real estate portfolio had stalled. She owned three properties, and for two years, nothing had changed. She had the equity, but not the strategy to use it. One evening, while reviewing her finances, she came across a discussion about AI-powered HELOC optimization systems. It claimed that investors were no longer using equity reactively but were instead using AI to design capital recycling strategies. At first, she didn't believe it. Equity, in her mind, was something you preserved—not something you constantly moved.

But curiosity got the better of her.

She entered her property details into an AI financing platform powered by advanced modeling tools similar to ChatGPT and a Mortgage Calculator system. Within seconds, the system analyzed her portfolio and presented something she didn't expect: a complete capital roadmap.

It showed her how much equity she could safely access across her properties. It then mapped out three different strategies. One was conservative, focused on slow expansion. Another was moderate, balancing risk and growth. But the third strategy stopped her cold.

It showed her how she could use her HELOC to fund the down payment on a DSCR rental property. That property would generate cash flow strong enough to support a second acquisition within eight months. Then, by refinancing one of her existing properties, she could restore her HELOC balance and repeat the cycle.

It wasn't just a loan plan.

It was a growth system.

Lena ran the numbers again and again. The AI didn't just show her what she could borrow—it showed her how capital could move through her portfolio like a continuous loop.

She hesitated. Borrowing against her home still felt risky. But the system didn't ignore risk. It simulated it. It showed her worst-case scenarios: rental downturns, rate increases, vacancy spikes. Even in those conditions, the strategy remained stable if executed correctly.

That gave her confidence.

She decided to move forward.

Her first step was simple. She opened a HELOC and accessed only a portion of her available equity. Instead of spending it, she followed the AI's recommendation exactly. She targeted a small duplex in a growing suburban market.

Within weeks, she closed the deal.

For the first time, she saw equity turn into motion.

Rental income began flowing in almost immediately. The system then updated her plan automatically. It showed her that within months, she would have enough cash flow stability to pursue another property. But the real transformation happened six months later.

Her HELOC balance had already been partially restored through structured repayment and rental surplus. The AI now recommended her next move: a second acquisition using the same strategy, but with a slightly optimized structure based on updated market conditions.

Lena realized something powerful.

Her portfolio was no longer static.

It was alive.

Capital was moving through it, growing it, reinforcing it.

She was no longer saving money and waiting for opportunity.

She was recycling opportunity itself.

One year later, Lena stood in front of five properties instead of three. None of it came from luck. None of it came from guessing. It came from structure.

And for the first time in her life, she understood what true leverage really meant.

It wasn't just borrowing against equity. It was learning how to make equity work like a system that never stopped building.

Chapter 4

Prequalification Intelligence and AI-Powered Approval Strategy

In traditional real estate investing, one of the most frustrating bottlenecks has always been the prequalification process. Investors often find a property, run the numbers, negotiate a deal, and then enter a long waiting period just to discover whether financing is even possible. This delay creates uncertainty, slows down decision-making, and in many cases leads to lost opportunities. Chapter 4 represents a major shift in this process, because artificial intelligence transforms prequalification from a reactive, document-heavy procedure into a predictive intelligence system that evaluates financing eligibility before an offer is even made.

The core problem with traditional prequalification is that it operates backwards. Investors identify opportunities first, then attempt to determine financing feasibility afterward. This approach creates inefficiency because time and emotional energy are spent on deals that may not qualify. AI reverses this structure by introducing prequalification intelligence at the earliest stage of the investment process. Instead of asking "Can I get approved for this loan?", investors begin by asking "Which deals am I most likely to get approved for, and under what structure?"

AI-powered prequalification systems analyze multiple dimensions of a borrower's financial profile simultaneously. Income streams, credit behavior, debt obligations, asset reserves, and property data are evaluated together rather than in isolation. This allows the system to generate real-time probability scores for different loan types, including conventional, DSCR, and Non-QM financing. Instead of waiting for a lender's interpretation, investors receive an immediate assessment of financing feasibility across multiple lending categories.

One of the most important advancements in this process is predictive underwriting simulation. Traditional underwriting occurs after a loan application is submitted, meaning investors have no insight into approval likelihood until later in the process. AI simulation models replicate underwriting logic in advance. They evaluate how lenders are likely to interpret income stability, rental projections, credit utilization, and reserve strength. This allows investors to see potential approval outcomes before engaging with lenders directly.

This predictive capability fundamentally changes how investors evaluate deals. Instead of falling in love with a property first and worrying about financing later, they now run financing simulations first. A deal is no longer just a property—it is a combined assessment of asset quality and financing probability. If a property cannot pass AI-driven prequalification thresholds, it can be eliminated early, saving time and reducing opportunity cost.

DSCR lending plays a central role in this new system. Because DSCR loans rely on property income rather than personal income, AI can rapidly estimate qualification likelihood by analyzing rental market data. It evaluates comparable rents, occupancy trends, and seasonal fluctuations to project income stability. Based on this, it calculates whether a property meets minimum DSCR thresholds required by lenders. This eliminates guesswork and prevents investors from pursuing properties that appear profitable on paper but fail to meet financing requirements.

Non-QM lending adds another layer of complexity that AI simplifies significantly. These loans vary widely between lenders, with different interpretations of bank statements, asset reserves, and income documentation. AI systems map borrower profiles against lender-specific guidelines, identifying not just whether approval is possible, but which lender is most likely to offer favorable terms. This removes the need for multiple manual applications and reduces the uncertainty that often surrounds alternative financing structures.

Prequalification intelligence also improves negotiation power. When investors understand financing probability in advance, they can make stronger offers with greater confidence. Sellers are more likely to accept offers from buyers who demonstrate clear financing readiness. This creates a competitive advantage in fast-moving markets where certainty is often more valuable than price alone. AI effectively turns financing clarity into a negotiation tool.

Another critical advantage of AI-driven prequalification is its ability to optimize borrower structure before submission. Instead of submitting raw financial data, investors can adjust their financial presentation based on lender interpretation models. AI may suggest shifting focus to certain income streams, restructuring debt presentation, or strengthening reserve documentation. This does not involve altering financial reality, but rather aligning presentation with underwriting expectations to improve approval probability.

Speed is another transformational benefit. In traditional systems, prequalification can take days or even weeks. During that time, market conditions can change, competition can increase, and deals can be lost. AI reduces this delay to minutes or hours. Investors can evaluate multiple properties in a single session and immediately determine which ones are financeable. This dramatically increases deal velocity and reduces friction in the acquisition process.

HELOC integration further enhances prequalification intelligence by introducing liquidity awareness into the approval model. Instead of evaluating loans in isolation, AI considers available equity, potential draw capacity, and liquidity positioning. This allows investors to understand not only whether they can qualify for a property, but how they can fund it strategically using multiple capital sources. In many cases, HELOCs become the bridge that turns a borderline qualification into a fully executable deal.

As investors scale, prequalification intelligence becomes a portfolio-level tool rather than a single-transaction analysis. AI can evaluate how new acquisitions impact overall borrowing capacity, debt ratios, and liquidity health. This allows investors to maintain sustainable growth without overleveraging or compromising financial stability. Every new deal is assessed not just on its individual merits, but on its impact on the entire portfolio structure.

The true transformation happening here is the shift from uncertainty to clarity. In traditional investing, financing uncertainty is accepted as part of the process. In AI-driven investing, uncertainty is minimized through simulation, prediction, and optimization. Investors are no longer waiting for approval—they are designing approval pathways before they even apply.

Ultimately, prequalification intelligence represents a fundamental shift in control. Investors are no longer passive participants in the lending process. They become active architects of their financial outcomes. By integrating DSCR analysis, Non-QM mapping, HELOC strategy, and predictive underwriting into a unified system, AI creates a financing environment where approval is not hoped for—it is engineered.

This chapter marks a turning point in the series. Once investors understand prequalification intelligence, they stop thinking in terms of "Can I get this loan?" and start thinking in terms of "How do I structure every deal so it is already approved before I submit it?"

That shift is where real scale begins.

"The Offer That Shouldn't Have Worked"

Jared had been losing deals for years, not because he lacked experience, but because financing always slowed him down.

He could analyze properties quickly, identify strong rental opportunities, and negotiate well with sellers. But every time he made an offer, he had to attach the same uncertain phrase: "subject to financing approval." And every time, that uncertainty weakened his position.

One afternoon, after losing yet another duplex to a cash buyer, Jared decided something had to change. He heard about AI-powered prequalification systems that could simulate loan approvals before applications were submitted. He was skeptical, but tired of guessing. So he decided to test it.

He entered his full financial profile into an AI system integrated with lending models similar to ChatGPT and a Mortgage Calculator engine. Then he added the details of three properties he was considering.

Within seconds, the system began generating something he had never seen before.

Not just loan options.

Approval probabilities.

Each property was analyzed through multiple financing lenses. Conventional loan likelihood was shown. DSCR approval probability was calculated based on projected rental income. Non-QM eligibility was evaluated using simulated bank statement analysis. Even HELOC-based funding strategies were mapped out to determine liquidity feasibility.

Jared leaned closer to the screen.

One of the properties he had almost given up on—the duplex that had just been taken by another investor—showed something surprising. The AI indicated that under a DSCR structure, he would have had a 92% approval probability. The reason he lost the deal was not financing failure. It was financing delay.

That realization hit him hard.

He had been choosing deals first and asking for approval later.

He had been doing it backwards.

Determined to change his approach, Jared ran a new property through the system. A small four-unit building in a rapidly growing area. Instead of focusing on price first, he focused on financing simulation first.

The AI broke it down instantly.

Conventional loan: moderate approval probability but slower timeline.

DSCR loan: high approval probability with strong cash flow alignment.

Non-QM option: viable but less optimal due to documentation structure. HELOC-assisted strategy: fastest execution with strong capital efficiency.

But what stood out most was something else.

The AI showed him that if he structured his offer using DSCR financing combined with a partial HELOC down payment, he could close faster than competing buyers who were relying on conventional financing.

For the first time, Jared didn't feel like he was chasing deals.

He felt like he was designing them.

He made the offer that same day.

This time, instead of writing "subject to financing," he wrote something different. He stated clearly that financing had already been prequalified through multiple lending scenarios, including DSCR approval modeling.

The seller accepted within 48 hours.

Jared was shocked. Not because he won the deal—but because he realized why he had been losing before.

It wasn't that he lacked financing options.

It was that he lacked financing intelligence.

Over the next month, Jared continued using the system. Before analyzing any property, he ran prequalification simulations first. He stopped wasting time on deals that didn't align with financing probability. Instead, he focused only on properties that the system identified as structurally strong across multiple loan types.

His closing speed increased. His confidence improved. And for the first time, sellers began responding differently to his offers.

They saw certainty.

Not hope.

Six months later, Jared had acquired three properties instead of one. Not because he found better deals—but because he stopped wasting time on deals he couldn't finance efficiently.

Standing inside one of his newly acquired units, he realized something simple but powerful.

He had not become a better negotiator.

He had become a better strategist.

And the difference wasn't effort.

It was intelligence applied before the offer was ever made.

Chapter 5

Borrower Optimization and AI-Driven Financial Positioning

At this stage of the AI Real Estate Financing Series, the investor is no longer simply choosing loans, comparing options, or prequalifying deals. They are now entering the most advanced layer of financing strategy: borrower optimization. This is where artificial intelligence shifts the focus away from passive qualification and toward active financial positioning. Borrower optimization is the process of structuring, presenting, and aligning financial data in a way that maximizes approval probability, improves loan terms, and expands access to capital. It is not about changing financial reality—it is about strategically organizing it so lenders interpret it in the most favorable and accurate way possible.

In traditional lending environments, borrowers submit financial documents and wait for interpretation. The lender controls the narrative. Income is evaluated in a rigid way, debt is categorized without context, and assets are often treated as static rather than strategic. This creates a disconnect between real financial strength and perceived financial strength. Many investors who are highly capable financially are either limited or delayed simply because their financial structure does not align with traditional underwriting models. AI changes this dynamic by reversing the flow of interpretation. Instead of the lender fully controlling how data is understood, AI helps the borrower pre-align their financial profile with lender expectations.

One of the core components of borrower optimization is income classification strategy. Different loan types interpret income in different ways. Conventional loans rely heavily on tax returns and W-2 documentation, while DSCR loans focus on property income, and Non-QM loans may accept bank statements or asset-based qualifications. AI analyzes all income streams and determines which classification produces the strongest underwriting outcome for each loan scenario. For example, business deposits may be more valuable in a bank statement loan than in a conventional structure. Rental income may carry more weight in DSCR underwriting than self-reported projections. AI identifies these relationships automatically and guides the investor toward the optimal documentation pathway.

Another critical aspect of borrower optimization is debt structuring intelligence. Debt is not viewed equally across all lending systems. Some lenders heavily penalize revolving credit utilization, while others place greater emphasis on installment debt ratios. AI evaluates all existing liabilities and models how each lender category will interpret them. It then suggests timing strategies for debt repayment, restructuring, or consolidation that improve approval probability without negatively impacting liquidity. In some cases, simply adjusting credit utilization before applying for a loan can significantly improve loan terms. AI identifies these opportunities in advance.

Asset positioning is another major factor in borrower optimization. Traditional underwriting treats assets as either present or absent, often focusing on total value without understanding liquidity behavior. AI introduces a more advanced model by analyzing asset types, liquidity timing, and reserve strength. It determines how different lenders weigh checking accounts, investment accounts, retirement funds, and business reserves. In some lending programs, liquidity is more important than total net worth. In others, long-term asset stability is key. AI aligns asset presentation with the specific logic of each lender, improving overall financing outcomes.

One of the most powerful advancements in borrower optimization is the concept of lender matching intelligence. Instead of submitting applications broadly and hoping for approval, AI maps borrower profiles to lender behavior patterns. Each lender has internal preferences, risk tolerances, and underwriting tendencies that are not always visible to the borrower. AI systems analyze historical approval data, guideline structures, and program requirements to identify which lenders are most likely to approve a specific financial profile. This transforms lending from a guessing process into a targeted strategy.

Documentation optimization is another area where AI provides significant leverage. Many loan denials or delays occur not because borrowers are unqualified, but because documentation is incomplete, misaligned, or presented inefficiently. AI reviews financial documents before submission and identifies gaps, inconsistencies, or opportunities for improvement. It may recommend reorganizing bank statements, clarifying income categorization, or strengthening reserve documentation. This reduces friction in underwriting and increases the likelihood of fast, clean approvals.

Borrower optimization also plays a critical role in timing strategy. The timing of a loan application can significantly influence approval outcomes. Interest rate environments, lender liquidity cycles, and market conditions all impact underwriting flexibility. AI tracks these variables and recommends optimal submission windows. In some cases, waiting a short period can improve approval terms dramatically. In other cases, acting immediately may be necessary to secure favorable conditions before market changes occur. When combined with DSCR and Non-QM financing strategies, borrower optimization becomes even more powerful. For example, a borrower may qualify marginally under a conventional structure but achieve stronger approval under a DSCR model when income is reclassified. Alternatively, a Non-QM bank statement loan may provide more flexibility for self-employed borrowers if deposits are structured correctly. AI evaluates these combinations holistically, ensuring that every financial decision supports the strongest possible lending outcome.

HELOC integration further enhances borrower optimization by introducing liquidity flexibility into the structure. AI evaluates how equity can be used to strengthen down payments, improve reserve positioning, or enhance loan-to-value ratios. In many cases, strategic use of HELOC funds can shift a loan from borderline approval to strong approval category. This creates a layered financing approach where multiple capital sources are coordinated to strengthen borrower positioning.

As investors scale portfolios, borrower optimization becomes increasingly important at the systemic level. Lenders evaluate not just individual properties, but overall borrower behavior, portfolio exposure, and leverage consistency. AI tracks these variables across multiple loans and ensures that new financing aligns with long-term portfolio health. This prevents overexposure, reduces risk clustering, and maintains borrowing capacity for future acquisitions.

Ultimately, borrower optimization represents a shift from passive financial identity to active financial design. Instead of being evaluated solely on fixed data points, investors begin shaping how their financial profile is interpreted. AI acts as the bridge between raw financial data and lender interpretation logic, ensuring that every application is positioned for maximum effectiveness.

The result is a profound shift in control. Investors are no longer subject to inconsistent underwriting interpretations. They are actively participating in how their financial strength is presented, understood, and approved. Financing becomes less about approval and more about alignment. And alignment becomes a strategic advantage that compounds across every future transaction.

Borrower optimization is not just a financing tactic. It is a financial intelligence framework. It allows investors to operate with precision in a system that was once unpredictable. And once mastered, it transforms lending from a barrier into a tool for accelerated wealth creation.

"The Application That Changed the System"

Monica had been investing in real estate for nearly a decade. She was successful by most standards—owning multiple rental properties, maintaining strong cash flow, and building equity steadily over time. But despite her success, she had one recurring frustration: financing never felt consistent. One lender would approve her easily, while another would question the same exact financial profile. She never understood why.

She assumed it was just part of the system.

Until everything changed.

One evening, after being declined for a loan she was confident she would receive, Monica decided to take a different approach. Instead of immediately applying again with another lender, she began researching why approvals varied so dramatically. That search led her to a concept she had never heard of before: borrower optimization using AI-driven financial positioning.

Skeptical but curious, she entered her full financial profile into an AI financing system integrated with advanced underwriting logic and tools similar to ChatGPT and Mortgage Calculator systems. She included income details, rental property data, credit profile, asset reserves, and existing debt structure.

Within seconds, the system began analyzing her financial identity—not as a static application, but as a dynamic profile.

Then it revealed something she didn't expect.

Her previous loan denial wasn't because she was unqualified.

It was because her financial data had been interpreted incorrectly for that specific lender's model.

The AI broke it down clearly. Her income structure was strong, but it was categorized in a way that did not align with that lender's underwriting preferences. Her assets were sufficient, but not presented in a way that highlighted liquidity strength. Her debt ratios were acceptable, but structured in a way that reduced perceived flexibility.

None of it meant she was a weak borrower.

It meant she was misaligned.

The system then generated a full optimization plan.

It showed her how to reclassify income streams for different loan types. It recommended which lenders were most compatible with her financial structure. It suggested how to reposition assets to improve reserve strength perception. It even identified timing adjustments that would increase approval probability significantly. Monica was stunned. For the first time, she realized something important.

She had not been rejected because of her finances.

She had been rejected because of presentation.

She decided to test the system.

A new investment property had just come on the market—a duplex in a stable rental area. Instead of rushing into a loan application, she ran borrower optimization first.

The AI provided three distinct financing strategies.

One conventional structure, moderately viable.

One DSCR structure, highly optimized.

And one Non-QM bank statement structure, designed specifically for her income profile.

But the most important insight was not the loan type.

It was how her financial data should be structured before submission.

She followed the system exactly. She adjusted how her income was documented. She organized her assets differently. She aligned her application with the lender category most compatible with her profile.

Then she submitted the application.

This time, everything moved differently.

No delays. No confusion. No additional document requests.

Within days, she was approved.

Monica sat in disbelief as she reviewed the final terms. Not only was she approved faster, but the structure was better than any loan she had previously received.

That's when it clicked.

Nothing about her financial situation had changed.

Only the way it was presented had changed.

Over the next few months, Monica applied borrower optimization to every deal she evaluated. She stopped guessing which lender to use. She stopped submitting applications blindly. Instead, she used AI to design her financial positioning before every submission.

Her approval rate increased dramatically. Her closing speed accelerated. And her confidence in financing grew stronger than ever before.

But the most surprising part came later.

Lenders began responding differently to her applications.

Her files were cleaner. Her approvals were faster. Her terms were stronger.

She wasn't just applying for loans anymore.

She was engineering them.

One afternoon, while standing inside her newest rental property, Monica reflected on how much had changed.

She realized something simple but powerful.

The difference between frustration and success was not income.

It was intelligence applied before submission.

And for the first time in her investing career, she wasn't hoping for approval.

She was designing it.

Chapter 6

AI Timing Strategy, Rate Cycles, and Market-Driven Financing Decisions

In real estate financing, timing is often the most underestimated variable, yet it is one of the most powerful determinants of long-term wealth creation. Investors tend to focus heavily on finding the right property or securing the right loan structure, while overlooking when to act. Chapter 6 introduces a critical evolution in AI-driven financing: timing strategy intelligence. This is where artificial intelligence begins to evaluate not only what financing options exist, but *when* those options should be executed for maximum advantage. In a shifting interest rate environment and constantly evolving lending landscape, timing becomes a strategic weapon.

Traditionally, investors made financing decisions based on immediate opportunity. If a deal looked good, they pursued financing regardless of broader market conditions. This reactive approach often led to suboptimal loan terms, higher interest rates, or missed opportunities to refinance under better conditions. AI changes this by introducing predictive rate cycle modeling. Instead of reacting to market conditions, investors can now anticipate them. AI analyzes historical rate trends, Federal Reserve policy signals, lender liquidity cycles, and macroeconomic indicators to estimate the most favorable financing windows.

One of the most important components of timing strategy is interest rate environment analysis. Interest rates directly impact purchasing power, cash flow, and long-term equity growth. AI systems track rate movement patterns and identify cyclical behavior that is not always visible to individual investors. This allows for strategic decision-making, such as accelerating purchases before anticipated rate increases or delaying refinancing until favorable rate shifts occur. Instead of guessing, investors operate with probabilistic insight into future rate environments.

Another critical aspect of timing strategy is loan sequencing intelligence. Many investors assume financing is a one-time event per property. In reality, financing is often a multi-stage process involving acquisition, stabilization, refinancing, and capital recycling. AI helps structure these stages in advance. For example, an investor might use short-term financing to acquire a property quickly, then transition into a DSCR loan after rental income stabilizes, followed by a refinance into a lower-rate structure once market conditions improve. AI sequences these steps based on projected timelines, ensuring each stage aligns with optimal financial conditions. Refinancing timing optimization is another powerful AI application. Traditionally, investors refinance when they feel rates are low or when they need liquidity. AI introduces a more precise approach by analyzing break-even points, rate differential thresholds, and long-term cash flow projections. It determines whether refinancing will actually improve financial outcomes or simply shift debt without meaningful benefit. In some cases, AI may recommend waiting months before refinancing to achieve significantly better long-term results. In other cases, immediate refinancing may be optimal to unlock equity or improve leverage positioning.

Market cycle intelligence is also a key component of AI-driven timing strategy. Real estate markets move in cycles influenced by supply and demand, interest rates, employment trends, and regional economic growth. AI evaluates these cycles and overlays them with financing conditions. This allows investors to understand not just property value trends, but how those trends interact with lending environments. For example, a rising property market combined with tightening lending standards may create urgency for acquisition, while a cooling market with loosening credit conditions may present refinancing opportunities.

DSCR lending is particularly sensitive to timing because rental income assumptions and market conditions fluctuate over time. AI helps investors determine when a property is most likely to meet DSCR requirements under optimal conditions. For instance, waiting until seasonal rental demand increases may significantly improve DSCR ratios. Similarly, entering a market just before rental rate increases can enhance long-term cash flow performance. Timing becomes a direct lever for loan qualification strength.

Non-QM lending also benefits from timing optimization. Lenders in this category often adjust guidelines based on market demand, liquidity conditions, and portfolio risk appetite. AI tracks these subtle shifts and identifies windows where qualification standards may be more flexible or where documentation requirements may be more favorable. This allows investors to time applications strategically rather than submitting them blindly during unfavorable lending cycles.

HELOC utilization timing is another major area of optimization. Drawing equity too early can reduce financial flexibility, while drawing too late can result in missed investment opportunities. AI evaluates both market conditions and portfolio readiness to recommend optimal HELOC activation points. It considers factors such as upcoming acquisition opportunities, renovation cycles, and liquidity requirements. In many cases, AI will recommend staged HELOC usage rather than full drawdowns, preserving borrowing capacity for future cycles.

Another advanced concept introduced in this chapter is financing momentum tracking. Momentum refers to the compounding effect of sequential financial decisions. When investors time financing correctly, each loan builds upon the previous one, accelerating portfolio growth. AI tracks this momentum by analyzing how each financing decision impacts future borrowing capacity, equity accumulation, and cash flow expansion. This allows investors to maintain continuous growth rather than experiencing periods of stagnation between transactions.

AI also introduces predictive opportunity alignment. Instead of reacting to deals as they appear, investors can forecast when their financing capacity will align with upcoming market opportunities. This creates a forward-looking investment strategy where capital readiness and market timing are synchronized. For example, AI may predict that a borrower will reach optimal leverage capacity within three months, coinciding with expected seasonal property market activity. This alignment increases acquisition efficiency and reduces missed opportunities.

Stress testing plays an important role in timing strategy as well. AI simulates different economic scenarios, including interest rate spikes, rental market downturns, and credit tightening conditions. These simulations help investors understand how timing decisions affect long-term portfolio resilience. In some cases, delaying a loan or acquisition may reduce risk exposure significantly. In other cases, acting quickly may protect against unfavorable market shifts.

Ultimately, timing strategy transforms financing from a static decision into a dynamic system. Instead of asking "Can I afford this loan?", investors begin asking "When is the optimal moment to execute this loan for maximum long-term benefit?" This shift elevates financing from a transactional activity to a strategic discipline.

The integration of AI into timing strategy represents one of the most sophisticated advancements in real estate investing. It allows investors to move beyond reactive behavior and operate with predictive intelligence. Financing is no longer just about approval or structure—it is about alignment with time, cycles, and opportunity flow.

Investors who master timing strategy are no longer just participants in the market. They become synchronized operators within it, executing decisions when conditions are mathematically and strategically optimal. This is where true leverage is created—not just through capital, but through time itself.

"The Deal That Waited for Him"

Ethan used to believe timing in real estate was mostly luck. Sometimes he got great rates. Sometimes he didn't. Sometimes deals worked out. Sometimes they didn't. He assumed it was just part of the business. But over time, he noticed something troubling. The investors who seemed to grow faster than him weren't necessarily finding better deals—they were just moving at the right time.

One evening, after missing out on a refinance opportunity that would have saved him thousands annually, Ethan decided to take a different approach. He had heard about AI systems that could analyze financing timing and predict optimal loan execution windows. Instead of reacting to the market, these systems supposedly helped investors anticipate it.

Curious and slightly skeptical, Ethan entered his full portfolio and financing history into an AI platform powered by advanced models similar to ChatGPT and a Mortgage Calculator system. He included his existing loans, property values, rental income, and equity positions.

Within moments, the system generated something unexpected.

A timeline.

Not just numbers—but a strategic map of his entire financing future.

It showed him when interest rate environments would likely shift. It showed him when refinancing opportunities would become most beneficial. It even showed him when his portfolio would naturally reach optimal borrowing capacity for expansion.

Ethan stared at the screen, confused at first. He had never thought of financing this way.

Then something stood out.

One of his properties had been refinanced six months earlier at a rate he thought was "good enough." But the AI simulation showed that if he had waited just four more months, he could have secured a significantly better rate, saving him thousands over the life of the loan.

That realization bothered him.

He hadn't made a bad decision.

He had made a premature one.

The system then shifted focus to a new opportunity—a small multifamily property he had been watching for weeks. The AI didn't just analyze the deal. It analyzed timing. It showed him that current interest rates were slightly elevated but projected to decline within a short window based on historical cycle patterns. It recommended a short-term acquisition strategy using flexible financing, followed by a refinance once the rate environment improved.

But the most important insight wasn't the loan structure.

It was the timing sequence.

Ethan had always thought success came from acting fast. The AI showed him that success actually came from acting *at the right moment*, even if that meant waiting.

For the first time, he didn't rush into an offer.

He paused.

He monitored the system.

Two weeks passed. Then three. The property was still available. Most investors had moved on, assuming financing costs were too high in the current environment.

Then the AI notification appeared.

Optimal execution window identified. Rates had shifted slightly downward. Lender liquidity conditions had improved. DSCR qualification thresholds were becoming more favorable in that market segment.

Ethan acted immediately.

He submitted the offer, structured exactly as the system recommended.

It was accepted.

But the real validation came months later.

Interest rates had dropped further, just as predicted. Ethan refinanced under improved conditions, reducing his monthly payment significantly and increasing cash flow.

For the first time in his investing career, he realized something profound.

He hadn't just bought a property.

He had timed a financial system.

And the difference between his past mistakes and his current success wasn't intelligence alone.

It was learning when *not* to act—and when to let the system show him the right moment to move.

Chapter 7

AI Portfolio-Level Financing Systems and Scalable Capital Architecture

At this point in the AI Real Estate Financing Series, the focus shifts from individual strategies—loans, borrower optimization, timing, and capital tools—to something significantly larger: portfolio-level financing systems. This is where real estate investing evolves from a collection of separate transactions into a unified financial ecosystem. Instead of thinking about one property at a time, the investor begins to think in terms of interconnected capital flows, leverage positioning, liquidity cycles, and long-term scalability. Artificial intelligence becomes the central coordination engine that allows all financing decisions to operate as one integrated system rather than isolated events.

In traditional investing, each property is treated as a standalone financial decision. One loan is evaluated independently from another, and equity is managed reactively rather than strategically. This fragmented approach limits growth because it fails to account for how one financing decision impacts future borrowing capacity. AI introduces a portfolio-level view where every loan, refinance, HELOC draw, and equity position is analyzed in relation to the entire financial structure. This creates a living system where capital is constantly moving, adjusting, and optimizing itself across multiple assets.

One of the most important components of portfolio-level financing is capital flow mapping. AI tracks how money enters, exits, and circulates within a real estate portfolio. This includes acquisition funding, rental income reinvestment, debt servicing, equity extraction, and refinancing cycles. Instead of viewing these as separate events, AI connects them into a continuous loop. This allows investors to see how capital deployed in one property can eventually fuel the acquisition of another, creating a compounding system of growth rather than isolated investments.

Another key advancement is leverage balancing intelligence. As investors scale, they often unknowingly concentrate risk in certain areas of their portfolio. Too much leverage in one property or one financing structure can create vulnerability. AI solves this by analyzing overall debt distribution, loan types, interest rate exposure, and equity concentration. It then recommends adjustments to maintain a balanced portfolio structure. This might include refinancing specific properties, reducing exposure in high-risk segments, or reallocating capital to stabilize long-term performance. Liquidity management becomes another critical layer of portfolio optimization. Many investors experience a situation where they are asset-rich but cash-poor, limiting their ability to act on new opportunities. AI helps solve this by forecasting liquidity needs across the entire portfolio. It evaluates upcoming loan maturities, expected cash flow, renovation cycles, and market opportunities to ensure that capital is available when needed. This prevents liquidity bottlenecks that often slow down portfolio expansion.

AI also introduces what can be described as borrowing capacity forecasting. Every financing decision impacts future borrowing potential. Taking on too much debt too quickly can reduce flexibility, while under-leveraging can slow growth. AI continuously calculates how current decisions affect future borrowing capacity across DSCR loans, Non-QM products, conventional financing, and HELOC availability. This allows investors to scale intentionally rather than unintentionally reaching financial ceilings.

Another powerful element of portfolio-level systems is refinancing orchestration. Instead of refinancing properties individually based on immediate need, AI identifies strategic refinance windows that maximize overall portfolio benefit. It evaluates interest rate cycles, equity accumulation timelines, and cash flow improvements across multiple properties simultaneously. In some cases, refinancing one property may unlock capital that improves the performance of an entirely different segment of the portfolio. AI connects these outcomes into a coordinated refinancing strategy rather than isolated transactions.

Cross-collateral intelligence also plays an important role in scalable financing architecture. Many lenders evaluate multiple properties together when determining risk exposure. AI identifies when cross-collateralization can be beneficial or when it may create unnecessary constraints. It evaluates how linking or separating assets affects borrowing power, liquidity flexibility, and long-term exit strategies. This allows investors to structure portfolios in a way that maximizes both growth potential and financial flexibility.

As portfolios grow, risk distribution becomes increasingly important. AI continuously evaluates exposure across geographic regions, property types, financing structures, and market cycles. This ensures that investors are not overexposed to a single market downturn or lending condition shift. For example, if too many properties rely on short-term financing or variable-rate structures, AI may recommend diversification into more stable long-term debt instruments. This creates resilience within the portfolio without sacrificing growth.

Another major innovation is predictive scaling simulation. AI can project how a portfolio will evolve over time based on different financing strategies. For example, it can simulate what happens if an investor aggressively uses HELOC funding to acquire multiple properties versus using conservative DSCR financing over a longer timeline. These simulations reveal not just financial outcomes, but structural differences in portfolio stability, cash flow consistency, and long-term equity accumulation.

This level of insight transforms decision-making from reactive to strategic architecture. Investors are no longer asking, "Should I buy this property?" They are asking, "How does this acquisition affect my entire financial system over the next 3, 5, or 10 years?" AI provides the answer by modeling portfolio evolution under multiple scenarios and identifying the most efficient path to scale.

Another critical concept introduced in this chapter is financing redundancy planning. In scalable systems, reliance on a single financing method creates vulnerability. AI helps investors diversify funding sources across DSCR loans, Non-QM structures, HELOC strategies, private lending, and refinancing cycles. This redundancy ensures that if one lending channel tightens or becomes less favorable, the portfolio can continue growing through alternative pathways.

Ultimately, portfolio-level financing systems represent the highest level of real estate investing strategy. It is no longer about individual deals or even individual loans. It is about designing a self-sustaining financial ecosystem where capital continuously moves, compounds, and reinvests itself with minimal friction. AI acts as the coordination layer that makes this complexity manageable and scalable.

The investor who reaches this level is no longer operating as a traditional borrower. They are operating as a financial system designer. Every decision is intentional. Every loan is part of a larger structure. Every property contributes to a long-term capital architecture that grows in efficiency over time.

This is the true power of AI in real estate financing: it does not just improve decisions—it connects them into a unified system that compounds wealth intelligently.

"The Portfolio That Started Thinking for Itself"

Nathan never planned to build a large real estate portfolio. At first, it was just one rental property. Then another. Then a small duplex he refinanced a year later. Each deal felt separate, like individual wins in a long game. But as the properties grew, something started to feel off. He was making money, but it didn't feel organized. Cash flow came in unevenly. Refinancing decisions were made based on immediate needs. And every new property felt like starting over from scratch. One day, after struggling to decide whether to refinance one of his properties or use equity for a new acquisition, Nathan came across something new—AI portfolio-level financing systems. The idea was simple but powerful: instead of analyzing loans and properties individually, the system could evaluate his entire portfolio as one connected financial structure.

He decided to try it.

Nathan entered all of his properties into an AI system powered by advanced financial modeling tools similar to ChatGPT and a Mortgage Calculator engine. He included loan balances, interest rates, rental income, equity positions, and cash flow data.

What came back changed everything.

Instead of showing him individual property reports, the system generated a portfolio map.

It displayed how each property was connected through debt, equity, and cash flow cycles. It showed how refinancing one property could unlock capital for another. It showed how HELOC usage in one asset affected borrowing capacity across the entire portfolio. It even projected how his portfolio would evolve over the next five years under different financing strategies.

Nathan stared at the screen in disbelief.

He had never seen his investments this way before.

Then the system highlighted something critical.

Two of his properties were overleveraged in short-term financing structures. This created unnecessary risk exposure during potential interest rate fluctuations. Another property had significant untapped equity that could be strategically deployed without increasing overall portfolio risk.

But the most surprising insight wasn't about risk.

It was about opportunity.

The AI showed him that by refinancing one property and adjusting HELOC usage on another, he could unlock enough capital to acquire two additional properties without increasing his monthly risk exposure.

Nathan had always believed expansion required sacrifice. More risk, more stress, more uncertainty.

But the system showed him something different.

Expansion could be structured.

It wasn't about working harder.

It was about designing smarter capital flow. He followed the recommendation.

First, he refinanced one property under improved DSCR conditions. Then he strategically accessed equity from another using a HELOC structure. Instead of spending or holding the capital, he deployed it into two new acquisitions identified by the system as high-efficiency additions to his portfolio.

Within months, everything changed.

His portfolio was no longer random.

It was synchronized.

Cash flow became more consistent. Equity growth became more predictable. And financing decisions became faster and clearer than ever before.

But the most surprising moment came six months later.

The AI system sent him a notification.

Portfolio optimization complete. New scaling capacity unlocked.

Nathan had never seen that message before. It showed him that due to improved leverage balancing and refinancing timing, his borrowing capacity had increased significantly without adding additional income or capital.

In other words, his portfolio had become more powerful simply by being structured correctly.

Standing in one of his properties one evening, Nathan realized something that changed how he thought about investing forever.

He was no longer managing individual properties.

He was managing a system.

And that system was no longer reacting to him.

It was evolving with him.

For the first time, he understood what true scale really meant.

Not more properties.

Not more loans.

But a financial architecture that could grow intelligently on its own.

Chapter 8

AI Financing Ecosystem Design and the Future of Autonomous Real Estate Capital

At this stage of the AI Real Estate Financing Series, the conversation moves beyond individual strategies, beyond even portfolio-level optimization, and into something far more advanced: the design of an AI-driven financing ecosystem. This is the point where real estate investing stops being a collection of decisions and becomes a self-adjusting financial system. Instead of the investor manually managing loans, refinancing, HELOCs, DSCR structures, and capital allocation, artificial intelligence begins to coordinate these elements as an integrated ecosystem that continuously adapts to market conditions, portfolio performance, and long-term wealth objectives.

In traditional investing, capital management is fragmented. Investors make decisions sequentially—first acquisition, then financing, then management, then refinancing. Each step requires attention, timing, and manual intervention. This creates inefficiency because each decision is made in isolation rather than as part of a continuous system. AI changes this by converting fragmented processes into interconnected financial workflows. Financing becomes a dynamic ecosystem where every action influences future outcomes, and every decision is optimized in real time based on portfolio-wide intelligence.

At the core of this ecosystem is autonomous capital orchestration. This concept refers to AI systems that not only analyze financing options but actively coordinate capital deployment across multiple properties and loan structures. Instead of the investor deciding when to refinance, draw equity, or apply for new financing, the system continuously evaluates market conditions, property performance, and lending environments to recommend or execute optimal capital actions. This creates a shift from manual decision-making to system-guided financial execution.

One of the most important components of ecosystem design is liquidity automation. Liquidity is the lifeblood of real estate investing, yet most investors manage it reactively. AI introduces predictive liquidity mapping, where future cash flow needs, debt obligations, and investment opportunities are forecasted in advance. This ensures that capital is always positioned correctly before it is needed. For example, if a future acquisition opportunity is likely, the system may recommend pre-positioning HELOC capacity or restructuring debt to free up borrowing power before the opportunity becomes available.

Another critical layer is adaptive financing routing. In a traditional model, investors choose a single loan type per property. In an AI ecosystem, financing becomes fluid. DSCR loans, Non-QM products, HELOC structures, and conventional financing options are evaluated simultaneously and dynamically adjusted based on changing conditions. If interest rates shift, the system may reroute financing strategy toward short-term leverage. If rental income increases, it may transition the asset into a more stable long-term loan structure. Financing becomes a living system rather than a fixed contract.

Risk balancing across the ecosystem is another core function. Instead of evaluating risk at the property level, AI evaluates risk at the system level. It analyzes exposure across interest rate variability, tenant stability, geographic distribution, loan maturity schedules, and leverage concentration. If risk becomes unevenly distributed, the system automatically recommends corrective actions such as refinancing, debt restructuring, or capital reallocation. This ensures that the portfolio remains stable even during market volatility.

AI also introduces predictive equity engineering. Equity is no longer treated as passive appreciation; it becomes an active tool for growth. The system tracks equity accumulation across all assets and forecasts when and where it can be most effectively deployed. Instead of waiting for manual refinancing cycles, equity is strategically repositioned across the portfolio to maximize return on capital. This allows investors to continuously recycle value rather than waiting for traditional liquidity events.

Another major advancement is cross-market synchronization. Real estate markets do not move uniformly. Different regions experience different cycles of growth, stagnation, and correction. AI systems monitor these variations and align financing strategies accordingly. For example, if one market is experiencing rising rents while another is stabilizing, the system may recommend shifting acquisition financing toward the stronger market while using refinancing opportunities in the stable market to extract equity. This creates a geographically intelligent capital strategy.

Autonomous refinancing cycles are also a key feature of AI financing ecosystems. Instead of refinancing based on manual review or personal judgment, the system continuously evaluates whether refinancing would improve portfolio performance. It calculates break-even points, rate advantages, and cash flow improvements across multiple properties simultaneously. When conditions are optimal, refinancing becomes a system-triggered event rather than a manual decision. This ensures that capital is always structured in its most efficient form. Another critical function is capital velocity optimization. Capital velocity refers to how quickly money moves through the investment system and generates returns. AI tracks this velocity across acquisitions, refinancing, rental income, and equity cycles. It identifies bottlenecks where capital is sitting idle or underutilized and recommends strategies to accelerate movement. This may include consolidating loans, restructuring debt, or reallocating equity to higher-yield opportunities. The goal is to ensure that every dollar is actively working within the system at all times.

As ecosystems scale, they begin to exhibit emergent behavior. This means that the system starts optimizing itself in ways that are not explicitly programmed by the investor. For example, improved cash flow in one part of the portfolio may automatically trigger new acquisition opportunities in another. Increased equity in one asset may unlock financing capacity across the entire system. These interconnected responses create a compounding effect that accelerates growth without proportional increases in effort.

The investor's role in this environment shifts dramatically. Instead of manually managing each decision, the investor becomes a system architect. Their primary responsibility is not execution but oversight—defining goals, setting risk tolerance parameters, and reviewing system recommendations. AI handles the operational complexity, while the investor focuses on strategic direction. This separation of roles is what allows scale to become sustainable.

Ultimately, AI financing ecosystems represent the final stage of evolution in real estate capital strategy. At this level, financing is no longer a tool used occasionally to support investments. It becomes the central nervous system of the entire portfolio. Every property, every loan, every equity position, and every cash flow stream is connected through a unified intelligence layer that continuously optimizes performance.

The result is a shift from active investing to autonomous wealth systems. Investors no longer chase opportunities—they operate within systems that continuously generate, evaluate, and execute opportunities on their behalf. Financing becomes self-regulating, adaptive, and increasingly intelligent over time.

This is the future of real estate investing: not individual deals, not even portfolios, but fully integrated financial ecosystems that think, adapt, and optimize capital continuously.

"The System That No Longer Needed Permission"

Evan had spent years building what he believed was a successful real estate portfolio. Ten properties, consistent cash flow, and steady appreciation had given him confidence that he was doing well. But despite the outward success, his day-to-day experience told a different story. Financing decisions were still stressful. Refinancing required constant monitoring. Equity was sitting idle in some properties while others were overleveraged. It felt like he was always managing problems instead of building momentum.

Everything changed the day he was introduced to the concept of an AI financing ecosystem.

At first, it sounded abstract—too advanced to be practical. But the idea of a system that could manage financing across his entire portfolio automatically intrigued him. Instead of thinking about loans one by one, he would be able to see everything as one connected financial structure.

He decided to try it.

Evan uploaded his entire portfolio into an AI system powered by advanced financial modeling tools similar to ChatGPT and a Mortgage Calculator-based analysis engine. He included property values, loan terms, interest rates, rental income, equity positions, and historical cash flow data.

For a moment, nothing happened.

Then the system began to build something.

Not reports. Not summaries.

A live financial ecosystem map.

He watched as every property in his portfolio was connected through capital flow lines. Debt structures were displayed as dynamic relationships. Equity was shown as active capital pools rather than static value. Cash flow was visualized as a continuous system of movement rather than individual income streams.

Then the system did something unexpected.

It began making recommendations across his entire portfolio simultaneously.

One property was flagged for refinancing based on upcoming rate conditions. Another showed excess equity that could be deployed into a new acquisition. A third property had inefficient debt structure that was limiting borrowing capacity across the entire system.

But what surprised Evan most was not the recommendations.

It was the timing.

The system was already preparing actions he had not even considered. It showed him that within the next 90 days, his portfolio would naturally unlock enough borrowing capacity to acquire two additional properties—if capital was repositioned correctly.

Evan leaned back in his chair.

For the first time, he wasn't being asked to make a decision.

He was being shown how the system would evolve.

Over the next few weeks, Evan began following the system's recommendations step by step. He refinanced one property exactly when the system indicated optimal timing. He activated a HELOC strategy on another to unlock liquidity. He restructured debt on a third property to improve portfolio-wide leverage balance.

Something unusual started happening.

The system began adjusting itself.

Each action he took created new opportunities. Improved cash flow triggered new financing capacity. Repositioned equity unlocked additional leverage options. Refinancing decisions reshaped future acquisition pathways.

It no longer felt like he was managing a portfolio.

It felt like the portfolio was responding to itself. Then came the moment everything changed. The system generated a new message:

"Autonomous optimization threshold reached. Portfolio now operating as a self-adjusting financial ecosystem."

Evan didn't fully understand what that meant at first.

But he understood the results.

His liquidity was higher than it had ever been. His borrowing capacity had increased without additional income. And two new acquisition opportunities had already been identified, pre-qualified, and structured within the system before he even began searching.

A few months later, Evan sat in one of his newest properties, watching tenants move in. He wasn't reviewing spreadsheets anymore. He wasn't calling lenders. He wasn't worrying about timing or approval delays.

The system handled all of it.

What struck him most was the realization that he was no longer "applying" for financing.

Financing was happening continuously around him.

Not as a series of applications. But as a living system that adjusted, optimized, and expanded without waiting for permission.

And for the first time in his investing career, Evan understood the real difference between owning properties... and operating a financial ecosystem that never stopped growing.

Chapter 9

AI Portfolio Management, Automation Systems, and Scalable Real Estate Operations

At this stage of the AI Real Estate Financing Series, the focus shifts from how investors acquire capital and structure deals to something even more critical for long-term success: how entire real estate portfolios are managed, operated, and scaled using artificial intelligence. This is where the investor transitions from being a deal operator to becoming a systems operator. Instead of manually tracking properties, payments, tenants, maintenance issues, financing cycles, and equity positions, AI introduces a centralized intelligence layer that manages the entire portfolio as a unified operational system. The result is not just efficiency—it is scalability without proportional effort.

In traditional real estate investing, portfolio management is fragmented. Each property operates as a separate unit with its own set of problems, financial performance metrics, and operational demands. Investors often find themselves reacting to issues as they arise rather than proactively managing the system as a whole. This reactive approach limits scale because time and attention become the bottleneck. AI changes this by integrating all operational, financial, and financing data into a single ecosystem where everything is monitored, analyzed, and optimized continuously.

One of the most important components of AI portfolio management is centralized financial intelligence. Instead of reviewing individual property statements, investors can now view their entire portfolio through a unified financial dashboard. AI aggregates rental income, debt obligations, cash flow, reserve levels, and equity positions across all assets. It then identifies patterns, inefficiencies, and opportunities that would be difficult to detect manually. This allows investors to make decisions based on total portfolio performance rather than isolated property metrics.

Another critical advancement is predictive cash flow management. Traditional investors often review cash flow after it occurs, treating it as a historical result. AI transforms cash flow into a forward-looking metric. By analyzing rent trends, vacancy probabilities, seasonal fluctuations, and expense patterns, AI can forecast future cash flow with increasing accuracy. This allows investors to anticipate shortfalls, prepare for reinvestment opportunities, and optimize liquidity positioning before issues arise. Maintenance prediction and asset lifecycle management also play a major role in AI-driven portfolio systems. Instead of waiting for repairs or emergencies, AI analyzes property age, maintenance history, tenant behavior, and environmental factors to predict when maintenance events are likely to occur. This allows investors to schedule repairs proactively, reduce unexpected costs, and maintain property value more efficiently. Over time, this creates a more stable and predictable portfolio performance structure.

Another key element is tenant behavior analysis and retention optimization. High turnover is one of the most costly aspects of rental property ownership. AI analyzes payment history, communication patterns, lease duration trends, and behavioral indicators to identify tenant satisfaction levels. It then recommends retention strategies such as lease adjustments, communication improvements, or pricing optimizations. By reducing turnover, investors increase long-term profitability and stabilize cash flow.

Financing integration within portfolio management systems is another major breakthrough. Instead of treating loans as separate financial obligations, AI connects all financing structures across the portfolio. DSCR loans, Non-QM loans, HELOCs, and conventional mortgages are analyzed together to evaluate total debt exposure and borrowing capacity. This allows investors to understand how one financing decision impacts the entire system. For example, refinancing one property may unlock borrowing capacity for multiple future acquisitions. AI ensures these relationships are visible and optimized.

Automation of capital deployment is another transformative feature. In traditional investing, capital deployment requires manual decision-making, market analysis, and lender coordination. AI automates this process by continuously scanning portfolio performance and external market conditions to identify optimal reinvestment opportunities. When excess liquidity is detected, the system can recommend or initiate capital deployment strategies aligned with investor goals. This reduces idle capital and increases portfolio velocity.

Another important aspect is risk monitoring and mitigation at scale. As portfolios grow, risk becomes more complex and interconnected. AI continuously evaluates exposure across interest rate risk, geographic concentration, tenant diversification, financing structures, and liquidity levels. If risk thresholds are exceeded in any category, the system recommends corrective actions such as refinancing, asset reallocation, or capital restructuring. This ensures long-term portfolio stability even during volatile market conditions.

AI also introduces scenario simulation for portfolio scaling. Investors can test different growth strategies before executing them. For example, they can simulate aggressive acquisition using HELOC leverage versus conservative DSCR-based expansion. They can model the impact of rising interest rates, rental market shifts, or refinancing cycles on their entire portfolio. This allows investors to choose strategies based on data-driven projections rather than intuition.

Another major advancement is automated reporting and decision intelligence. Instead of manually reviewing spreadsheets or property reports, investors receive AI-generated insights that summarize portfolio health, identify risks, and recommend strategic actions. These insights are not static—they evolve as market conditions and portfolio performance change. This creates a dynamic feedback loop where decision-making becomes faster, more accurate, and more aligned with long-term objectives.

As portfolios scale further, AI introduces multi-layer optimization. This means decisions are no longer optimized at the property level or even portfolio level alone, but across multiple dimensions simultaneously. For example, a refinancing decision may improve cash flow, increase borrowing capacity, and reduce risk exposure all at once. AI evaluates these outcomes together to identify the most efficient path forward. Ultimately, AI portfolio management systems represent the final stage of operational efficiency in real estate investing. At this level, investors are no longer managing properties—they are managing systems that manage properties. The investor's role becomes strategic oversight rather than operational execution. This shift removes the traditional bottleneck of time and allows scaling to continue without proportional increases in workload.

The result is a fully integrated real estate operation where financing, maintenance, cash flow, tenant management, and capital deployment are all coordinated through a single intelligence layer. This is not just automation—it is systemization at scale.

Investors who reach this level are no longer constrained by manual management limitations. Their portfolios become self-regulating systems that continuously optimize themselves based on data, performance, and market conditions.

This is the foundation of true scalability in modern real estate investing.

"The Portfolio That Ran Without Friction"

Michael had built his real estate portfolio the old-fashioned way—one property at a time, one loan at a time, one tenant issue at a time. For years, it worked. He had grown to eight rental properties and considered himself successful. But as the portfolio grew, so did the complexity. What once felt manageable began to feel overwhelming. Maintenance issues stacked up. Financing decisions became harder to track. Cash flow fluctuated more than he expected. And despite owning more assets, he felt like he had less control.

One evening, after spending hours reviewing spreadsheets and tenant emails, Michael realized something uncomfortable. He wasn't managing investments anymore. He was managing problems.

That was the moment he began exploring AI portfolio management systems.

He connected his entire portfolio into an AI platform powered by advanced modeling systems similar to ChatGPT and a Mortgage Calculator-based financial engine. He expected reports. What he received instead was something far more advanced.

A live operational map of his entire real estate portfolio.

Every property was displayed as a connected node within a larger system. Cash flow moved between assets like a flowing network. Debt structures were visualized as interconnected financial pathways. Maintenance schedules appeared as predictive timelines rather than reactive tasks. Tenant behavior was analyzed and categorized automatically. Michael sat in silence for several minutes just observing it.

Then the system began speaking to him through insights.

It identified two properties that were draining liquidity due to inefficient financing structures. It highlighted one property where refinancing would unlock capital without increasing risk. It flagged another property where tenant turnover risk was increasing based on behavioral patterns he had never noticed before.

But what struck him most was not the problems.

It was the clarity.

For the first time, everything was visible.

Over the next few weeks, Michael began following the system's recommendations. He refinanced one property exactly when the system indicated optimal timing. He adjusted rent strategies based on AI pricing recommendations. He scheduled maintenance proactively instead of reactively. He restructured financing on two properties to improve portfolio-wide liquidity.

Something unexpected began happening.

The portfolio started to stabilize. Cash flow became more consistent. Expenses became more predictable. Financing decisions became easier. Even tenant turnover decreased.

But the biggest change wasn't financial.

It was psychological.

Michael was no longer reacting to problems.

He was operating within a system that prevented them.

Then came the moment that changed everything.

One morning, the AI system generated a portfolio summary update:

"Operational friction reduced by 68%. Portfolio stability threshold achieved. Scaling capacity unlocked."

Michael didn't fully understand what that meant at first.

But the results were clear.

He now had enough borrowing capacity to acquire two additional properties without increasing his risk exposure. The system had already identified them, analyzed them, and pre-qualified financing structures for both.

He hadn't searched for deals.

The system had prepared them. A few months later, Michael stood inside one of his newest properties. Tenants were moving in. The property was already cash-flow positive. Financing had been seamless. Maintenance systems were already scheduled. Everything felt... effortless.

He realized something powerful.

He wasn't managing a portfolio anymore.

He was overseeing a system that managed itself.

And for the first time in his investing career, he understood what true scale really meant.

Not more work.

Not more stress.

But less friction... and more intelligence running the entire operation beneath him.

Chapter 10

The Fully Autonomous AI Real Estate Empire — Building a Self-Running Wealth System

At this final stage of the AI Real Estate Financing Series, everything comes together into one unified concept: the fully autonomous AI real estate empire. This is where financing, deal sourcing, underwriting, portfolio management, capital recycling, timing strategy, borrower optimization, and operational systems are no longer separate disciplines. Instead, they merge into a single intelligent architecture that continuously builds, adjusts, and scales itself. The investor is no longer operating as a participant in the system—they are operating as the architect of a self-sustaining wealth engine that functions with minimal manual intervention and maximum strategic control.

In traditional real estate investing, even advanced investors remain bound by manual workflows. They search for deals, evaluate financing, coordinate with lenders, manage tenants, track expenses, and make strategic decisions in isolation. Each step requires attention and time. As portfolios grow, this manual structure becomes increasingly difficult to scale. The limiting factor is no longer opportunity—it is operational bandwidth. AI removes this limitation by converting every stage of the real estate process into an interconnected system that communicates, adapts, and optimizes in real time.

At the foundation of the autonomous empire is AI-driven deal generation intelligence. Instead of manually searching for properties, investors rely on systems that continuously scan markets, identify undervalued assets, and rank opportunities based on financing feasibility, cash flow potential, and long-term appreciation. These systems integrate data from MLS feeds, off-market databases, rental analytics, and economic indicators. The result is a constantly updating pipeline of opportunities that are already filtered through financing and profitability models before the investor ever sees them.

The next layer is autonomous financing orchestration. In a traditional model, financing is reactive and manual. In an AI-powered empire, financing is continuously optimized across multiple lending structures simultaneously. DSCR loans, Non-QM products, conventional mortgages, HELOC strategies, and hybrid financing systems are all evaluated in real time. The system determines which structure produces the best combination of cash flow, leverage efficiency, and long-term scalability. It can even sequence financing events across time, ensuring that refinancing, acquisitions, and equity extraction occur in the most efficient order possible.

Borrower optimization evolves further at this stage into identity-based financial structuring. Instead of simply improving loan applications, AI continuously refines how the investor's entire financial identity is presented to the lending ecosystem. Income classification, asset positioning, credit behavior, and liability structure are all dynamically adjusted within legal and ethical boundaries to align with evolving lender models. This creates a continuously optimized borrower profile that adapts to different lending environments without requiring manual restructuring for each transaction.

Portfolio intelligence becomes fully autonomous in this phase. Every property is no longer managed individually but exists as part of a unified financial organism. Cash flow, debt obligations, maintenance cycles, tenant behavior, and equity positions are all tracked in real time. AI systems detect inefficiencies and automatically recommend or execute adjustments that improve overall system performance. Underperforming assets are flagged for refinancing, repositioning, or divestment, while high-performing assets are leveraged for expansion and capital recycling.

Capital recycling reaches its highest level of efficiency in the autonomous model. Equity is no longer extracted sporadically—it is continuously evaluated and strategically deployed across the portfolio. When sufficient equity accumulates in one area, AI redirects it toward acquisition opportunities, debt optimization, or liquidity strengthening. This creates a perpetual motion system where capital is constantly moving, compounding, and reinvesting without stagnation.

Timing intelligence becomes fully predictive at this stage. Instead of reacting to interest rate changes or market cycles, AI forecasts optimal financing windows, acquisition timing, and refinance opportunities across the entire portfolio. These predictions are based on macroeconomic data, lender behavior patterns, seasonal real estate cycles, and internal portfolio performance. The system ensures that every major financial decision is executed at the point of maximum advantage, reducing risk and increasing long-term returns.

Risk management evolves into systemic stabilization. Rather than identifying risk after it occurs, AI continuously simulates potential future scenarios across the entire portfolio. Interest rate shocks, market downturns, tenant disruptions, and liquidity constraints are modeled in advance. When vulnerabilities are detected, the system automatically recommends structural adjustments such as refinancing, diversification, or capital reallocation. This creates a resilient financial ecosystem that adapts before instability occurs.

At the highest level, the AI real estate empire operates as a closed-loop wealth generation system. Deal flow feeds financing models. Financing models feed acquisition decisions. Acquisitions feed portfolio performance. Portfolio performance feeds capital recycling. Capital recycling feeds new acquisitions. Every component reinforces the next, creating a self-sustaining cycle of growth. The investor's role becomes less about execution and more about setting strategic parameters, defining risk tolerance, and overseeing system direction.

This is where the true transformation occurs. Real estate investing is no longer a collection of isolated activities. It becomes a living financial architecture that operates continuously. The investor is no longer trading time for money or effort for returns. Instead, they are designing systems that generate, optimize, and expand wealth autonomously over time.

The fully autonomous AI real estate empire represents the endpoint of financial evolution within this framework. It is not about doing more deals or managing more properties. It is about building a system that thinks, adjusts, and grows independently within defined strategic boundaries. Once this system is established, scale is no longer limited by time, attention, or operational capacity. Instead, scale becomes a function of system intelligence.

And wealth becomes a function of system design.

"The Empire That No Longer Needed a Manager"

When Adrian started investing in real estate, he thought success meant owning properties. For years, he worked toward that goal—finding deals, securing loans, managing tenants, and slowly building a small portfolio. At first, it felt empowering. He was in control, making decisions, and watching his investments grow. But as the portfolio expanded, something changed. The system he had built began demanding more from him than he could realistically give.

Every day was filled with decisions. Should he refinance this property? Should he raise rents? Should he use his HELOC for a new acquisition? Which lender should he choose? Which deal should he prioritize? The more he grew, the more complex everything became. He wasn't scaling freedom—he was scaling responsibility.

One evening, after spending hours trying to coordinate financing for three different properties at once, Adrian reached a breaking point. He realized he wasn't building wealth anymore. He was managing chaos.

That was the moment he discovered AI-driven real estate ecosystem systems. At first, he didn't believe it. The idea that an entire portfolio could be managed as a unified system sounded unrealistic. But curiosity pushed him forward. He entered every detail of his portfolio into an advanced AI platform powered by systems similar to ChatGPT, integrated with financing intelligence, portfolio modeling, and real estate analytics tools.

Then he waited.

What came back was not a report.

It was a system map.

His entire portfolio was visualized as a living financial structure. Each property was connected through capital flows, debt relationships, and cash flow cycles. Financing structures were displayed as dynamic systems that adjusted over time. Equity was not static—it moved, expanded, and reallocated across assets.

Then the system began analyzing itself.

It identified inefficiencies in his financing structure that he had never noticed. It showed him that two of his properties were underleveraged while another was overexposed to interest rate risk. It highlighted unused HELOC capacity that could unlock two additional acquisitions immediately. It even projected how his portfolio would evolve over the next three years if optimized correctly.

Adrian felt something unfamiliar.

Clarity.

For the first time, he wasn't guessing.

He was observing.

Over the next several weeks, Adrian followed the system step by step. He refinanced properties exactly when the system indicated optimal timing. He reallocated capital from underperforming assets. He used equity strategically instead of emotionally. Every decision was coordinated through the AI ecosystem rather than made independently.

Something unusual began happening.

The system started improving itself.

Each action he took created new opportunities. Increased cash flow triggered new borrowing capacity. Optimized financing unlocked additional acquisition pathways. Risk adjustments stabilized portfolio performance, which further increased scalability.

Then came the moment that changed everything.

The system generated a notification: "Autonomous portfolio behavior achieved. Human intervention no longer required for operational continuity."

Adrian stared at the message for a long time.

It wasn't saying he was irrelevant.

It was saying the system no longer depended on manual management.

A few months later, Adrian found himself doing something he hadn't done in years.

He wasn't reviewing deals.

He wasn't negotiating loans.

He wasn't managing tenants or coordinating financing.

Instead, he was reviewing system recommendations.

The AI had already identified new properties, structured financing options, optimized equity usage, and mapped out expansion pathways.

All he had to do was approve strategy direction.

One afternoon, Adrian walked through one of his newest properties. Tenants were moving in. The financing had been seamless. The numbers were already optimized. Everything felt stable without his involvement.

He realized something profound.

He wasn't running a real estate business anymore.

He was overseeing a system that ran itself.

And for the first time, he understood what true financial freedom actually meant.

It wasn't owning properties.

It wasn't managing investments.

It wasn't even building wealth.

It was building a system so intelligent, so coordinated, and so self-adjusting that wealth creation continued—even when he stopped actively managing it.

Final Comments

The End of Manual Real Estate Investing and the Beginning of Intelligent Capital Systems

Reaching the end of this series is not an ending in the traditional sense. It is a transition point. Everything covered throughout these chapters was designed to move you from a fragmented, manual approach to real estate investing into a fully integrated, AI-driven financing and portfolio system. The goal was never just to teach you how to find deals, analyze properties, or get better loans. The goal was to fundamentally change how you think about capital, leverage, timing, and scale. Because in the modern real estate landscape, success is no longer defined by effort alone. It is defined by systems—systems that think, adapt, and optimize faster than any individual ever could manually.

If you reflect on where most investors start, the pattern is always the same. They begin with enthusiasm, learning how to find properties and run numbers. Then they move into financing, often facing confusion, delays, and inconsistent lender feedback. Over time, they begin to understand that real estate is not just about properties—it is about capital structure. But even then, most investors remain trapped in reactive decision-making. They wait for approvals, respond to lender conditions, and adjust strategies based on external constraints rather than internal systems. This is where the limitation has always existed. Not in opportunity, but in coordination.

Artificial intelligence removes that limitation. It does not replace the investor. It replaces inefficiency. It removes fragmentation. It eliminates the delays between insight and execution. And most importantly, it connects every part of the real estate process into a single unified system. Deal flow, financing, underwriting, borrower positioning, capital recycling, portfolio management, timing, and risk are no longer separate disciplines. They become one continuous loop of intelligence.

One of the most important shifts introduced throughout this series is the idea that financing is not an event—it is a system. Traditional investors treat loans as isolated transactions. They apply, wait, and accept terms. But AI reveals something deeper: every loan is connected to future loans, every financing decision affects future borrowing capacity, and every structure influences long-term portfolio scalability. Once you see financing as a system rather than an event, your entire approach to investing changes permanently.

Another critical shift is the understanding that timing is not luck—it is information. Interest rates, lender behavior, market cycles, and refinancing windows are not random. They follow patterns that can be analyzed, predicted, and strategically leveraged. AI makes these patterns visible. It transforms timing from guesswork into strategy. Investors who once acted based on urgency can now act based on optimal conditions. This alone changes the trajectory of long-term wealth building.

Borrower optimization introduces another layer of transformation. Most investors assume that financing outcomes are fixed based on income and credit. But what AI reveals is that outcomes are heavily influenced by how financial data is structured and interpreted. Income classification, asset positioning, debt presentation, and documentation strategy all influence lender perception. When optimized correctly, the same investor can achieve dramatically different financing results without changing their actual financial strength. This shifts control back to the investor, where it belongs.

Portfolio thinking is perhaps the most important evolution of all. Instead of viewing each property as a separate investment, AI encourages investors to see their entire portfolio as one interconnected financial organism. Cash flow, equity, debt, and liquidity are not isolated—they are interconnected variables within a larger system. When one part of the system is optimized, it impacts everything else. This creates compounding effects that traditional investors rarely experience because they are focused on individual transactions rather than systemic design.

Capital recycling is the mechanism that turns portfolios into growth engines. Instead of allowing equity to remain idle, AI identifies opportunities to continuously redeploy capital into new acquisitions, refinancings, or debt optimizations. This creates a cycle where capital is never static. It is always moving, always generating new returns, and always contributing to portfolio expansion. Over time, this compounding effect becomes the difference between linear growth and exponential scale.

Risk management also evolves significantly with AI integration. Traditional investors often discover risk after it has already impacted their portfolio. AI reverses this process by simulating risk scenarios before they occur. Interest rate changes, market corrections, tenant disruptions, and liquidity constraints are modeled in advance. This allows investors to adjust proactively rather than reactively. Risk becomes something that is continuously monitored and mitigated rather than something that surprises the system.

As these systems mature, something even more powerful emerges: autonomy. Not in the sense that the investor becomes irrelevant, but in the sense that the system becomes capable of operating without constant manual input. Deals are evaluated continuously. Financing options are optimized dynamically. Portfolio performance is monitored in real time. Capital is allocated based on predictive models. The investor transitions from operator to architect, from manager to strategist, from executor to system designer.

This is the true evolution of real estate investing in the age of artificial intelligence.

Not more effort.

Not more complexity.

But less friction, more intelligence, and greater scalability.

However, there is one final truth that must be understood clearly. AI does not guarantee success. It amplifies structure. If the system is poorly designed, AI will accelerate inefficiency. If the investor lacks discipline or clarity, AI will scale confusion. But if the investor builds with intention, strategy, and long-term thinking, AI becomes one of the most powerful wealth-building tools ever created in the history of real estate.

The opportunity now is not just to participate in the market. It is to redesign how participation itself works. To move from reacting to structuring. From guessing to modeling. From managing to systemizing. And from isolated decisions to integrated intelligence.

This series was never just about loans, properties, or tools. It was about a mindset shift. A shift from manual investing to intelligent systems. From individual transactions to capital ecosystems. From effort-based income to structured wealth architecture.

If you understand that shift, then you understand the future of real estate.

And more importantly, you understand your role in it.

Because in this new environment, the investors who win are not the ones who work the hardest.

They are the ones who build systems that no longer depend on constant manual control.

Systems that think.

Systems that adapt.

Systems that scale.

And systems that continue building wealth long after traditional effort has stopped.

www.ingramcontent.com/pod-product-compliance
Ingram Content Group UK Ltd.
Pitfield, Milton Keynes, MK11 3LW, UK
UKHW010012031026
15589UKWH00008B/1617

9 798295 885303